[architec

[architecture and hygiene]

ADAM KALKIN

batsford

[(4)colophon]

[All rights reserved] [No part of this publication may be reproduced in any form without written permission from the publisher] [British Library cataloguing in publication] [A CIP record for this book is available from the British Library] [Published by B T Batsford] [A member of Chrysalis Books plc] [64 Brewery Road London N7 9NT] [www.batsford.com] [First published 2002] [Copyright © Adam Kalkin 2002] [ISBN 0 7134 8789 5] [Printed in Italy by G. Canale & C. S.p.A.] [For a copy of the Batsford catalogue or information on special quantity orders of Batsford books please contact us on 020 7697 3000 or sales@chrysalisbooks.co.uk]

[contents(5)]

[epigraph 6] [introduction 7] [bunny lane house 8] [clown comic strip 24] [gun misses unemployed clown 25] [untitled contact sheet 26] [motion-sensitive heater 27] [geoff tabin memorial sculpture 28] [balloons 30] [dog lifter 31] [implantable telephone 32] [farm house, new jersey 33] [coffin interior design 37] [new york city loft 38] [electrical tower conversion 40] [scaffold house or twenty-six-room house 42] [baby monitor piece 44] [mommie, I am sorry 45] [tar and feathers 50] [casco show 52] [project for leipzig 53] [smoking norma 54] [one bird teaching another bird to speak 55] [bicycle-powered electric chair 56] [shimanski test 58] [bombs 60] [against modernism 62] [the solution to your problems 64] [sole film 65] [$99,000 house 66] [mail-order bride 72] [collector's house 74] [jetway house 84] [$101,000 house 85] [house for matt and anne 86] [moveable house 90] [philosophy of furniture 92] [sphincter of loneliness 94] [car museum 98] [mik cadillac 100] [stereophonic rumble strips 101] [house for a hollywood producer 102] [garage door screen patent 104] [video gravestone 106] [adam with ina 110] [jerry with ina 111] [dead dogs in coffee 112] [store fixtures 113] [rolling wardrobe 114] [playground in the form of the rolling wardrobe 116] [multi-family housing 118] [martha's vineyard house 120] [tenement 130] [house for a monk 132] [$102,000 house 134] [fireworks dense 135] [100 comments on architecture and hygiene 136] [picture credits 140] [afterword 141]

[(6) epigraph]

Once something is said (made explicit) it emerges from the shadows of the unseen into the realm of the possible. Therefore, we must be careful of what we say. Even when we just think something, the entire world of potentialities re-arranges itself.
—William James, *Selected Letters*

Only 20 per cent of architecture is skin or visible surface. The rest is flesh. In this book, I perform a rather unscientific vivisection of my thoughts on architecture, cutting through bone here, an artery there, fat occasionally. Such are the difficulties of surveying a living organism with primitive surgical technique.
—Adam Kalkin, 2001

[(8) bunny lane house]

The cottage was already on the site.
Interior decoration by Albert Hadley.

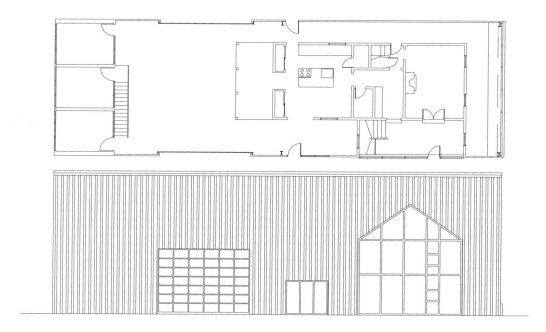

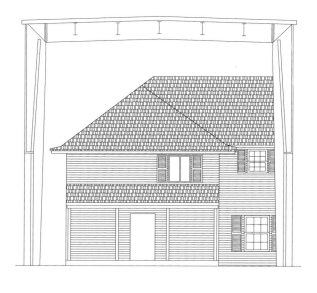

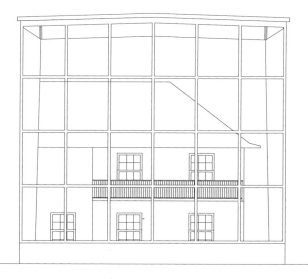

Better,

phone rings,
gun misses unemployed clown
(number is listed)

The balloons nod encouragement when the heater gets turned on automatically by the visitor.

[(28) geoff tabin memorial sculpture, 2000]

This piece converts the Casco Gallery in
Utrecht into an operative brothel.
The artist keeps 20% of the revenues, the
gallery 10%, and the girls the rest.

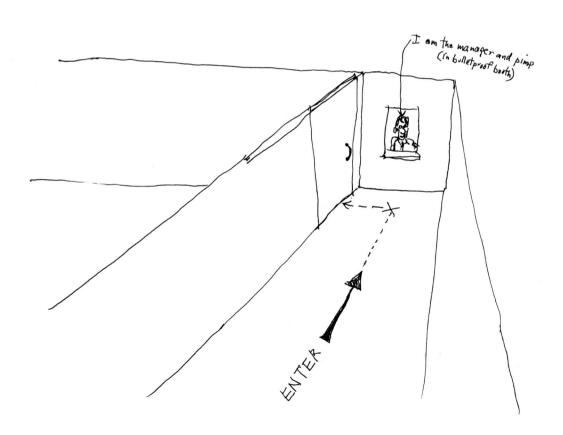

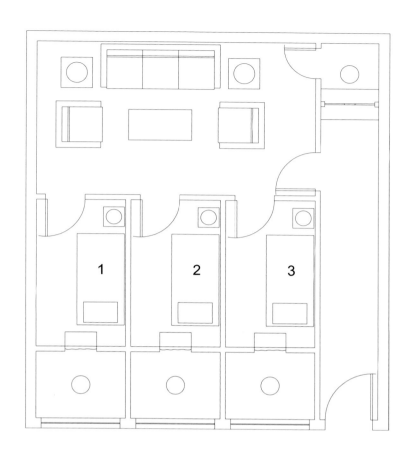

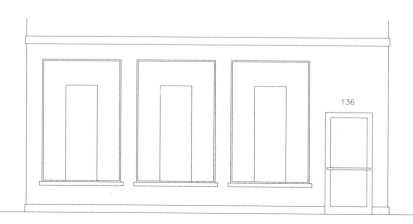

136

[dog lifter, 1992 (31)]

With Aernout Mik.

receiver is wired directly into neurons

transmitter is cemented to jaw bone

[farm house, new jersey, 1990–2000 (33)]

The original house in 1966.

Concrete addition completed in 1990.

Louvered addition completed in 2000.

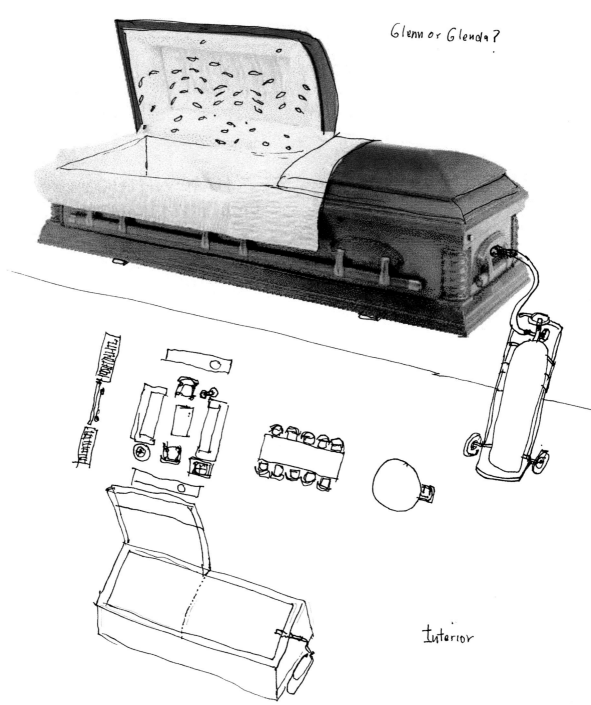

Glenn or Glenda?

Interior

[(38) new york city loft, 1990]

[(40) electrical tower conversion, 2001]

Electrical towers are under-utilized public
spaces. Converted to multi-family
housing, they create a new kind of suburb.

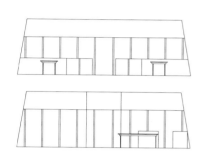

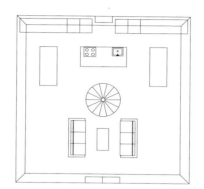

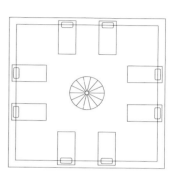

[(42)scaffold house or twenty-six-room house, 2001]

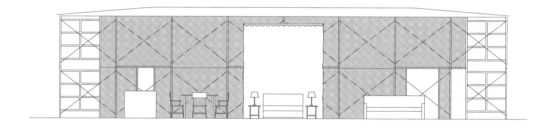

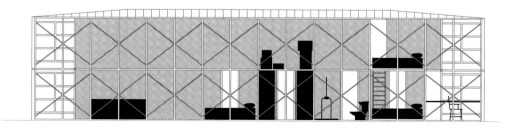

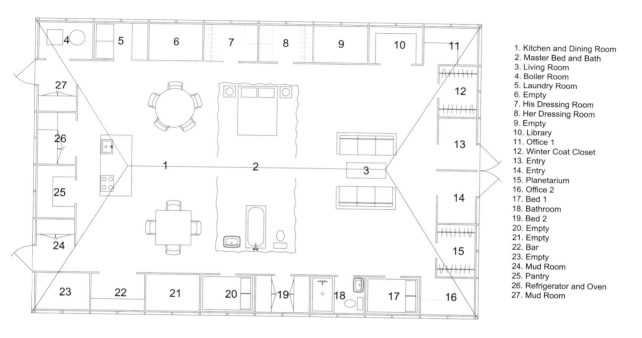

1. Kitchen and Dining Room
2. Master Bed and Bath
3. Living Room
4. Boiler Room
5. Laundry Room
6. Empty
7. His Dressing Room
8. Her Dressing Room
9. Empty
10. Library
11. Office 1
12. Winter Coat Closet
13. Entry
14. Entry
15. Planetarium
16. Office 2
17. Bed 1
18. Bathroom
19. Bed 2
20. Empty
21. Empty
22. Bar
23. Empty
24. Mud Room
25. Pantry
26. Refrigerator and Oven
27. Mud Room

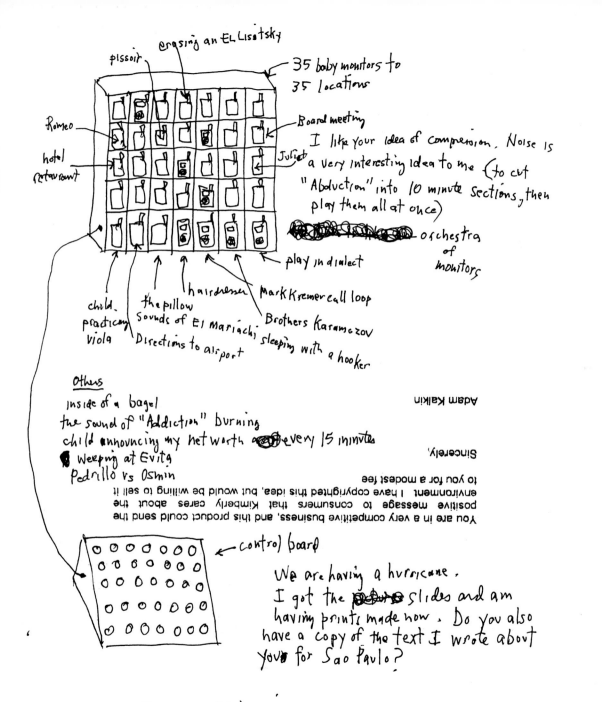

erasing an EL Lisetsky

pissoir

35 baby monitors to 35 locations

Romeo

hotel restaurant

Board meeting

I like your idea of compression. Noise is a very interesting idea to me (to cut "Abduction" into 10 minute sections, then play them all at once)

Juliet

orchestra of monitors

play in dialect

child practicing viola

the pillow

Sounds of El Mariachi

Directions to airport

hairdresser

Mark Kremer call loop

Brothers Karamazov sleeping with a hooker

Others

inside of a bagel

the sound of "Addiction" burning

child announcing my net worth every 15 minutes

Weeping at Evita

Pedrillo vs Osmin

control board

We are having a hurricane. I got the slides and am having prints made now. Do you also have a copy of the text I wrote about your for Sao Paulo?

Adam Kalkin

Sincerely,

to you for a modest fee
environment. I have copyrighted this idea, but would be willing to sell it
positive message to consumers that Kimberly cares about the
You are in a very competitive business, and this product could send the

In nova fert animus

[m o m m i e, I a m s o r r y, 1 9 9 5 (45)]

Events take place at various locations
around the world at various times
according to a central schedule.
With Aernout Mik in Middelburg.

	A	B	C	D	E	F	G
1	dog				perfume 1		
2			boot		perfume2	mommie	
3							
4			dog	cookies		mommie	
5				cookies			
6	bell			cookies		mommie	
7	bell			cookies			
8	bell				inflatable	mommie	
9	bell		gases	cookies	perfume 3		
10							mommie
11	bell		boot	cookies	inflatable		
12	bell	suitcase	toothbrush	cookies	inflatable	mommie	
13	bell	suitcase		policeman	perfume 4		
14	heist	suitcase		cookies	perfume 5	mommie	bricks
15	bell				perfume 6		
16	diesel musician					mommie	chess genius
17							
18	bell		boot		dog	mommie	boot
19	bell			baptism			boot
20	bell			carpet		mommie	
21	bell	suitcase			weltschmertz	girl in bag	
22	bell		fraud		perfume 7	mommie	chess genius
23							
24					inflatable		
25		suitcase	boot			mommie box	
26		lemonface			inflatable	mommie box	
27						mommie box	
28						mommie	
29							
30						mommie	

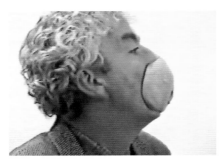

[$_{(50)}$tar and feathers, 1992]

With Aernout Mik.

[(52) casco show, 1994]

Visitors pay 5 guilders for the right to
blow a dart at the balloon wall.
Some balloons contain a gift certificate.
When a balloon is popped, the winner is
entitled to a prize: a massage, a stock
certificate, a sample of the artists' DNA,
a dose of ether, etc...
With Berend Strik in Utrecht.

Project for Leipzig;

① mouse in rocket powered car

② drives off tall building

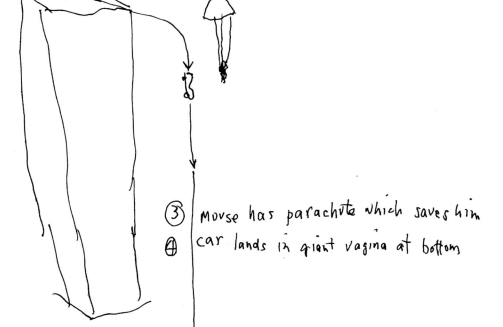

③ Mouse has parachute which saves him
④ car lands in giant vagina at bottom

All this is filmed by 4 carefully placed
cameras and relayed to audience in
a coffee shop.

[(54) smoking norma]

Every ten minutes Smoking Norma
belches 100 cubic feet of smoke into
the gallery.
With Berend Strik.

[one bird teaching another bird to speak₍₅₅₎]

A mechanical parrot teaches a live parrot to say 'Hello, Shimanski!' and 'Mirabelle Dictu!'

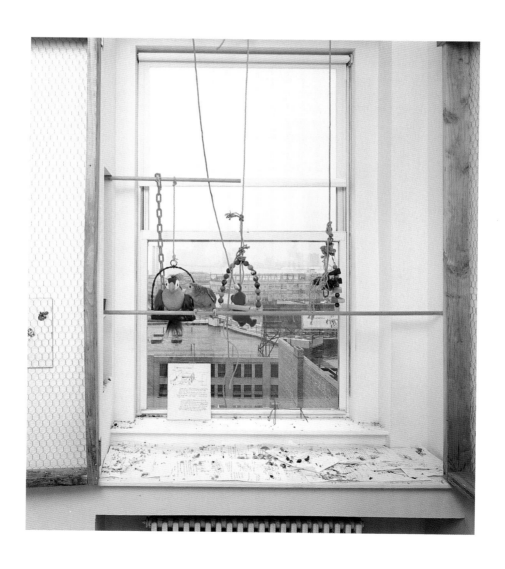

[(56) bicycle-powered electric chair, 2000]

This performance requires two participants: one to pedal the bicycle, the other to be electrocuted. The audience may volunteer either to pedal or to be electrocuted. Those who do not wish to volunteer may participate in the compensation plan. Pedalers will be paid on an hourly basis. Those being electrocuted will be paid based on the total voltage that his or her body absorbs. The generator is calibrated so that the maximum voltage will stop short of death.

pedalling electric chair

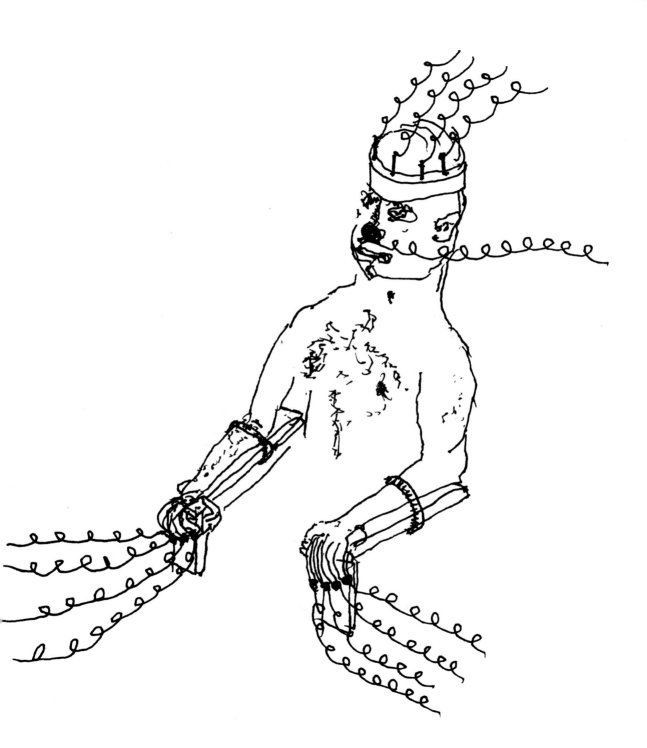

[(58) shimanski test, 1999]

Mr Shimanski, a cheap-suited
apparatchik, administered this test
to visitors. In the adjacent room, a clown,
a prostitute and a bird danced to the
music of Jimi Hendrix.
With Berend Strik in New York City.

NAME: _____ AGE:_____
　　　　　　last　　　　　　　first

DATE:_____ / _____ / _____　　　EDUCATION:_____

MULTIPLE CHOICE: CIRCLE ONE CHOICE ONLY

Diaper is to Sari as:
a) urbanism is to classicism　b) rain is to fog　c) fez is to spanking

Who was the <u>least</u> well-known:
a) Plotinus　b) Elvis　c) The Nancy Drew Series

FILL IN THE BLANK:

Tarkovsky made only black and white films because he suffered from _____.

Glenn Gould _____ Jerry Lewis.

TABLE TOP PROBLEM: INDICATE CHOICE BY POINTING ONLY

Which vessel contains more liquid ?

VERBAL SECTION: ONE HOUR TIME LIMIT

Compare and contrast the major works of Martin Landau with those of Lester Young.

TIMED EVENT:

Arrange the blocks in a Latin Cross.

ESSAY: WRITE TWENTY WORDS OR LESS ON THE FOLLOWING TOPIC

Clinton: Sage or Bedwetter?

EXTRA CREDIT: OPTIONAL

Would you rather be gagged by velvet soaked in Martin Landau's urine or be "kept" by Andrew Lloyd Webber?

plug in parcel #1

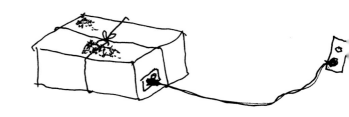

Bombs

Designed to explode on inflame in specific dramatic sequence.

Bomb #1 (the "Punctus")

a) Latex model of the artist's nose heats up, burns, then combusts which
b) Ignites a drop of gasoline
c) pasta explosion inside a scale model of the Tze-tze Palace

Remains: the eyeballs of IL Duce "

Bomb #2

Designed to match the personality of the recipient.
It has two parts: a synthetic fur chamber which contains the leaves of an African Violet, a small vial of "Diamond Creme" perfume and a pillow stitched by Berend Strik.

Second part: the head of a cat stuffed with vaseline and hemp.

Sequence:

```
•- - -    15 seconds
plug in                    •  33 seconds  thick smoke
               Intriguing odor      •  - - - - - -  - ✗
                                        10 seconds    Gelatinous
                                                      explosion
```

Bomb 3:

```
•- - -    1 minute
plug in                    o  - - -      36 hours
            release of                              - - - •
            insects                                 Sour milk
```

[(62) against modernism, 1991]

Each day, the hallway shortens itself until
the visitor is ejected into the street.

The Solution to Your Problems

Used Ocean Cargo Containers

The international trade industry invested millions of dollars to design a cargo/storage container capable of protecting valuable merchandise from theft, damage, and weather in transit. You can now buy a "high-tec" container for a fraction of its original cost. There is nothing else like it!

Virtually Vandal Proof

SIZES
8x8x40'
8x8x20'

Instant Building On Your Lot
No Site Preparation Required. We Can Deliver And Place On Ground. Use It Immediately

CONTAINERS AVAILABLE
THROUGHOUT THE U.S.A. & HAWAII
WE CAN ARRANGE DELIVERY

CALL FOR QUOTES

DRY CARGO CONTAINERS
Used / New - also known as Milvans
Approximate size - 8' X 8 1/2' X 20'
1097 cubic feet or 35,000 lbs.
Approximate size - 8' X 8 1/2' X 40'
2265 cubic feet or 64,000 lbs.

Containers are fabricated out of 14 gauge steel. Frame is made out of minimal 6-8 gauge steel. Doors located at rear with hinges and 4 knuckle locking bars with hasps, * one knuckle locking bar on right door may have a 1/4" continuous weld locking system box. Box is designed to prevent the use of bolt cutters or hack saw. Made to use for padlock devices.

Containers have approximately 1" hardwood floors which are treated against insects and rodents.

Used containers can be sandblasted and painted upon request. Containers can be lifted by crane or fork lift by going underneath container.

* Option

Insulated And Refrigerated
Units available

Used – Refrigerated Units
Refrigerated containers are ideal for any walk-in cold storage application (temporary or permanent, in-plant or outdoors).
230 V. – 3 Phase – 3 1/2 " Insulated Walls.

Delivery $250⁰⁰

SPECIFICATIONS

$2595⁰⁰

Storage Container 20 Foot
Dimensions:
Length: 20'
Width: 8'
Height: 8'6"

Storage Container 40 Foot
Dimensions:
Length: 40'
Width: 8'
Height: 8'6"

AZTEC TECHNOLOGY CORP.

Serving Continental U.S.A. and Hawaii

CALL TOLL FREE

1-800 624-8045

Paul Arends

 WE ALSO ACCEPT:

4/94 2k

[sole film, 2002 (65)]

This patent sections the sole of a sneaker into razor-thin layers, each of which bears an image. As the sole wears, the successive underlying images are exposed, creating a very slow-motion film.

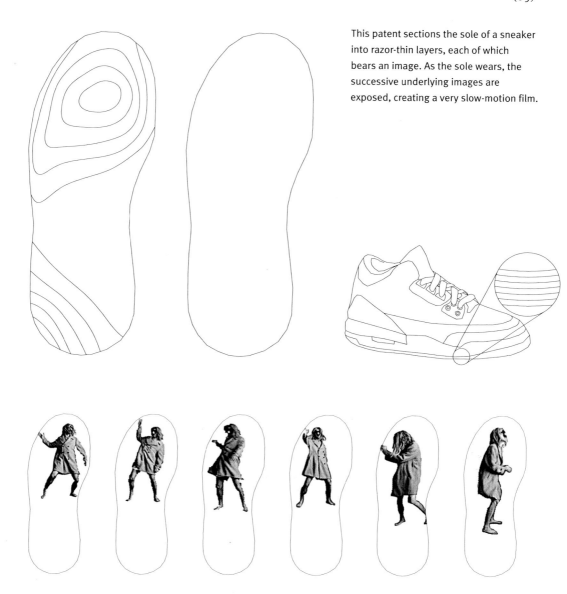

[(66) $99,000 house, 2001]

Buy this house by calling (001) 908 696 1987.

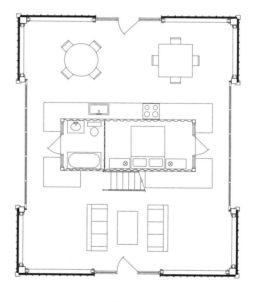

1st Floor Plan

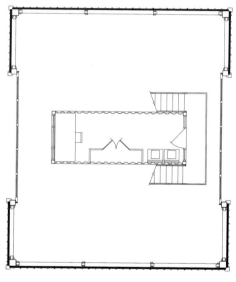

2nd Floor Plan

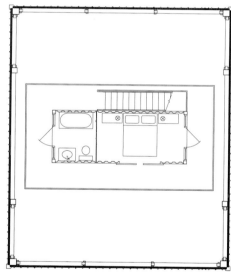

3rd Floor Plan

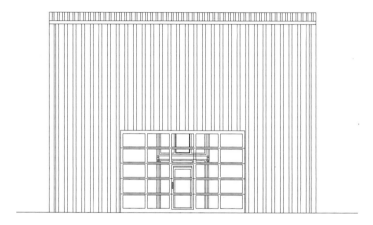

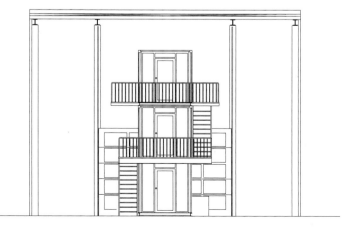

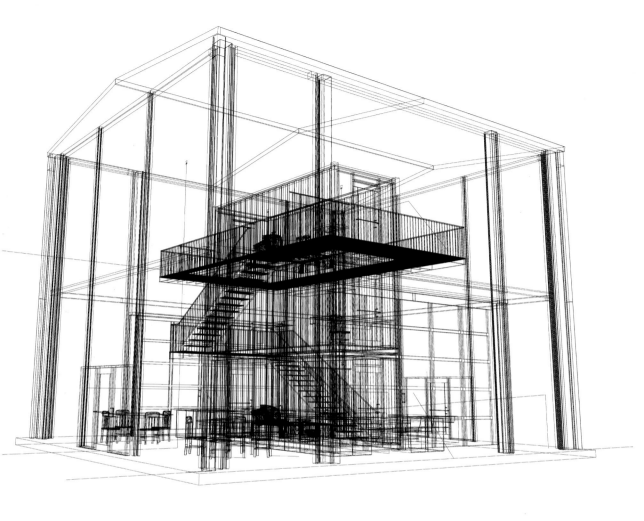

[$_{(72)}$mail-order bride, 2ooo]

Darkness is a powerful emollient for love.
This piece immerses two lovers in total
blackness during the first month of their
intimacy.

keh enters here

Name: Larissa Tolokonnikova
Country(city): Russia (Ozersk)
Age : 37
Date of birth : 8th of March, 1964
Weight (kg) : 52
Height (cm) : 166
Marital status : divorced
Children : yes, daughter of 17 years old
Languages : some English
About me : I am benevolent, friendly, loyal, patient,
romantic and the optimist with good sense of humour.
I enjoy sport: a bicycle, riding, skates, table tennis,
billiards, car. I adore to read detectives, to listen to
music, to prepare tasty baking. I am a nurse, medical
laboratory assistant
Looking for : I am looking for honest, ungloomy, not
losing heart man, who wants to be happy together with
me.

KEN

enters here

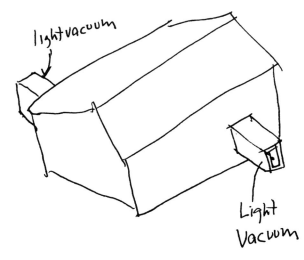

lightvacuum

Light
Vacuum

[₍₇₄₎ collector's house, 2001]

Shelburne Museum, Shelburne, Vermont.
A house for a fictional collector of folk art.
The house is made from shipping
containers and other found objects. It is
decorated by Albert Hadley with art from
the Shelburne Museum collection.

[(84) jetway house, 2001]

A driveable glass protuberance.

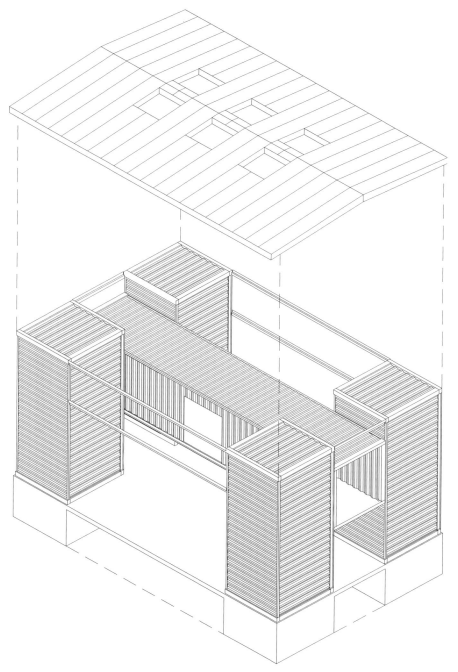

[(86)house for matt and anne, 2001]

Made from 12 shipping containers.

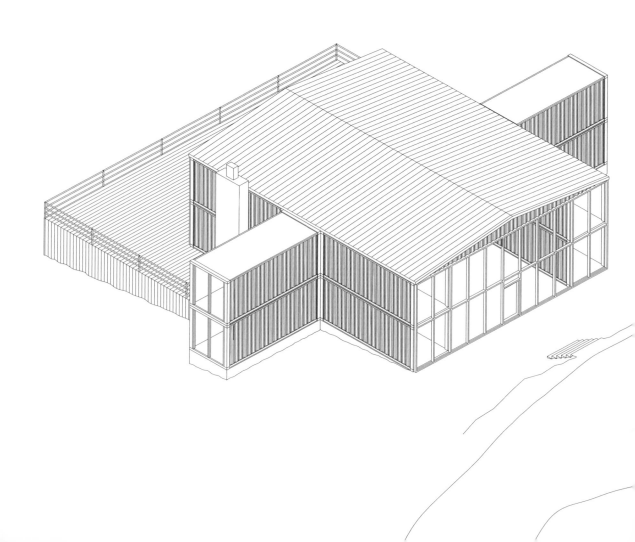

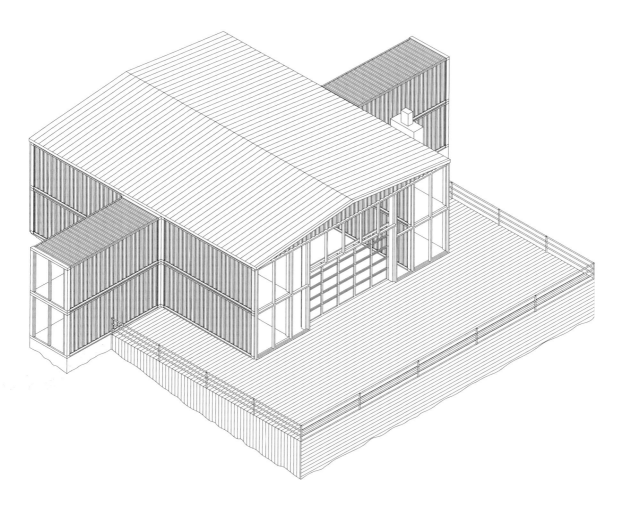

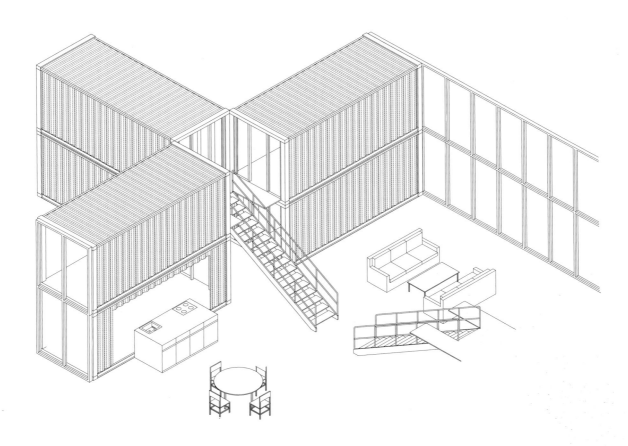

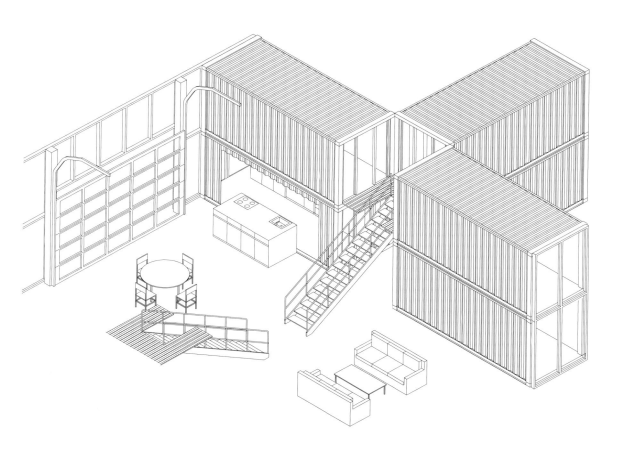

[(90) moveable house, 2001]

The house rests on six slim posts. It can
be moved around a site on the whim of
its owners.

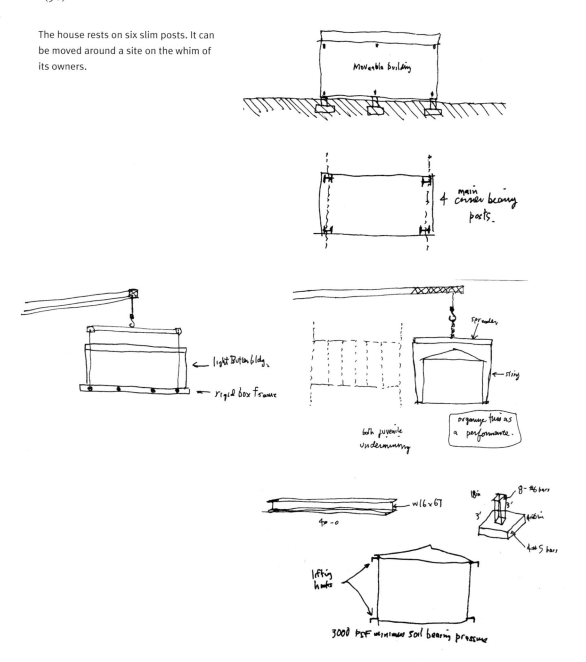

Moveable Building

4 main corner bearing posts.

light Butler bldg.

rigid box frame

both juvenile
undermining

spreader

sling

organize this as
a performance.

W16 x 67

40' - 0

lifting
hooks

18in

8 - #6 bars

3'

3'

4 #5 bars

3000 PSF minimum soil bearing pressure

Vittorio Gregotti,

I spoke to the guy at Butler Manufacturing Co.. He thinks we can move
a 30' x 40' x 18' bldg. with a crane like this:

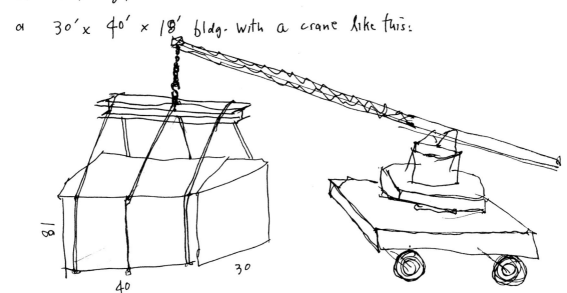

[(92) philosophy of furniture, 1992]

Installation based on Edgar Allan Poe's
essay of the same title.
With Aernout Mik in Amsterdam.

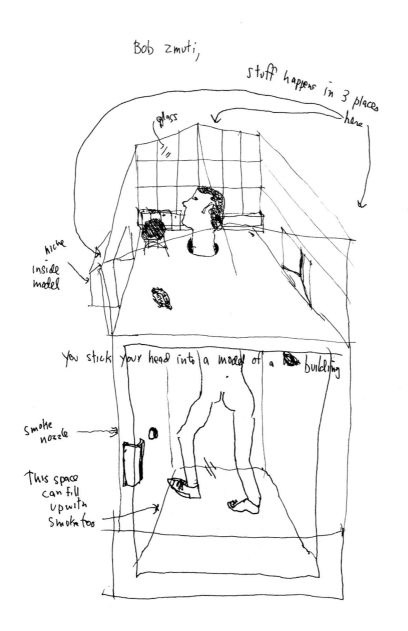

Bob zmuti,

glass

stuff happens in 3 places

here

niche - inside model

you stick your head into a model of a building

smoke nozzle

This space can fill up with smoke too

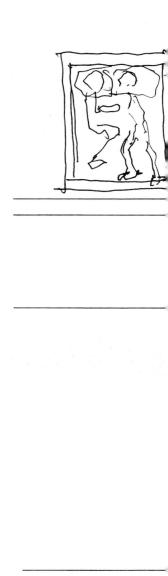

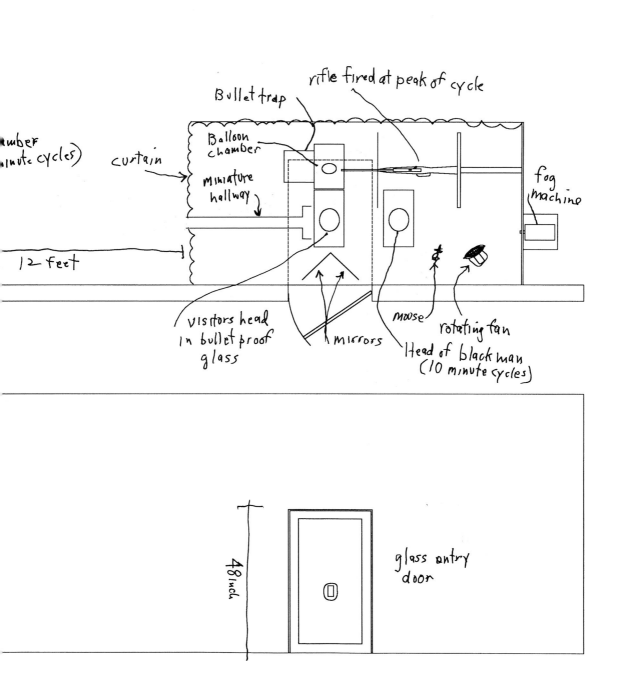

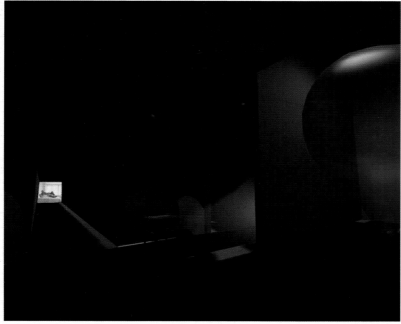

[(98) car museum, 2001]

The Car Museum fits in any urban parking
space. It travels from city to city with
its miniature collection of site-specific
art works.

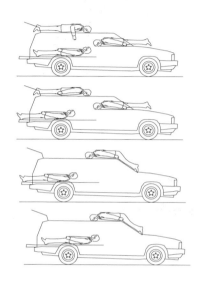 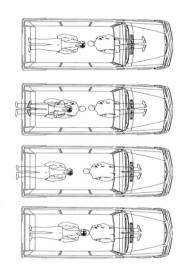

window is
flat screen video monitor
(flying kick)

man # 2

man #2
back
here

hose for
sucking

tires are filled
with NO_2
(laughing
gas)

Aernovt, this is a Volvo - Should we ask Volvo to actually make one
of these?

Mom - You can see pictures of the Shelburne house: www.shelburnemuseum.org
click on Collector's House

[(100)mik cadillac, 1996]

Part of a campaign to sell Aernout Mik's
work in Florida. I sat in the car every day
for one month answering questions
about it. At the end I gave the car to the
American Lung Association.

[stereophonic rumble strips, 2001 (101)]

This patent application is designed to introduce music to long stretches of the Federal highway system. Rumble strips of various musical frequencies are etched into the roadbed. When traveling at the speed limit, the right tires of the car will play the melody and the left tires will play the bass rhythm. Billboards will announce the title and composer of each piece.

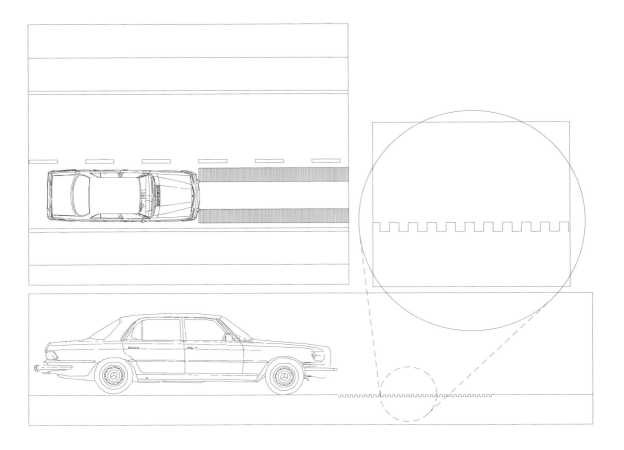

[(102) house for a hollywood producer, 2001]

In Hollywood, one's potency is measured
by the extravagance of one's cars. In this
house, the owner is surrounded by his
cars in glass garages.

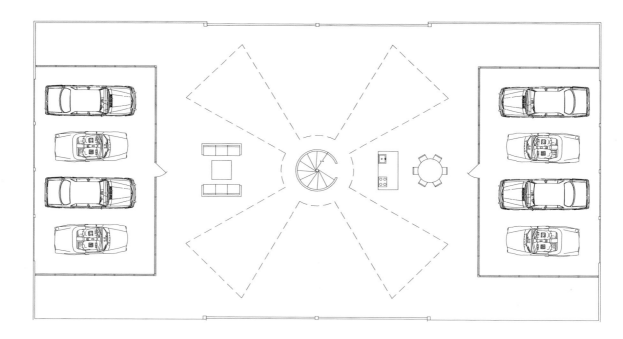

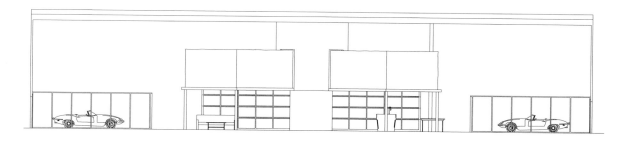

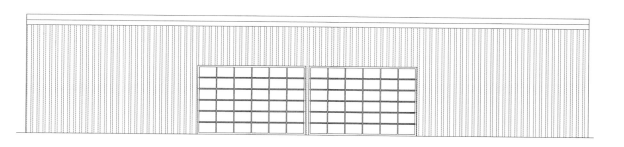

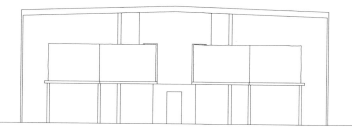

[(104) garage door screen patent, 2001]

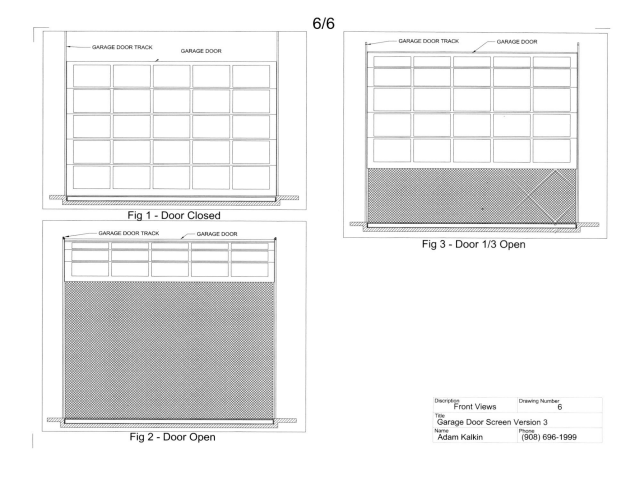

Fig 1 - Door Closed

Fig 2 - Door Open

Fig 3 - Door 1/3 Open

Discription		Drawing Number
Front Views		6
Title		
Garage Door Screen Version 3		
Name	Phone	
Adam Kalkin	(908) 696-1999	

5/6

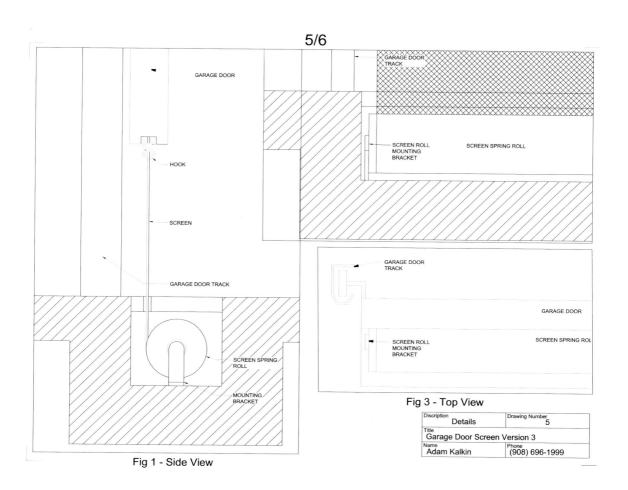

GARAGE DOOR

GARAGE DOOR
TRACK

HOOK

SCREEN ROLL
MOUNTING
BRACKET

SCREEN SPRING ROLL

SCREEN

GARAGE DOOR TRACK

SCREEN SPRING
ROLL

MOUNTING
BRACKET

Fig 1 - Side View

GARAGE DOOR
TRACK

GARAGE DOOR

SCREEN ROLL
MOUNTING
BRACKET

SCREEN SPRING ROL

Fig 3 - Top View

Discription	Details	Drawing Number	5
Title	Garage Door Screen Version 3		
Name	Adam Kalkin	Phone	(908) 696-1999

[₍₁₀₆₎ video gravestone, 2001]

In this patent application, each headstone
is equipped with a flat-screen video
monitor which plays clips from the
deceased person's life.

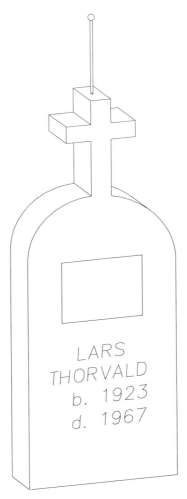

wirelss video signal

secure signal
for Catholics

press this button to
begin video

TOM MIX

BORN 7·17·41
DIED 4-12-81

MARY M.

MODIGLIANI

14·11-91

graveyard welcome
center

Video
message"
from dead
person

Unit with eyepiece for private viewing

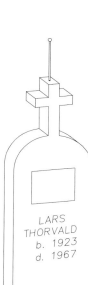

LARS
THORVALD
b. 1923
d. 1967

LARS
THORVALD
b. 1923
d. 1967

LARS
THORVALD
b. 1923
d. 1967

LARS
THORVALD
b. 1923
d. 1967

Adam with Ina.

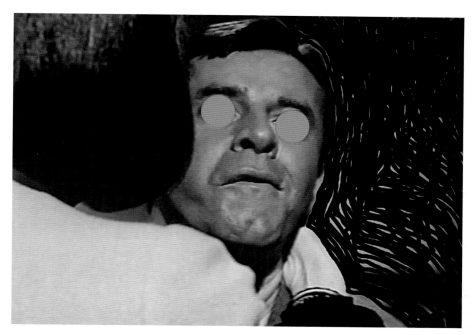

Jerry with Ina.

[(114) rolling wardrobe, 1992]

[(116) playground in the form of the rolling
wardrobe, 1993]

Site.

Model.

[(118) multi-family housing]

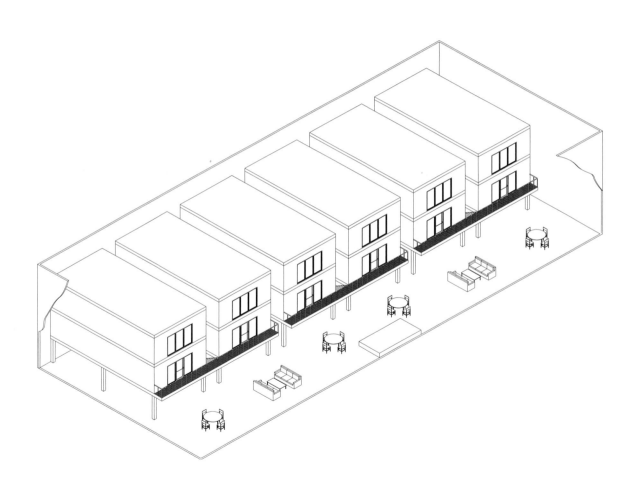

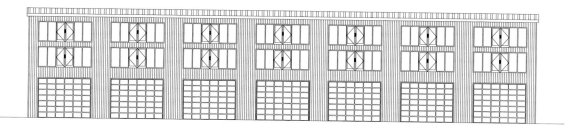

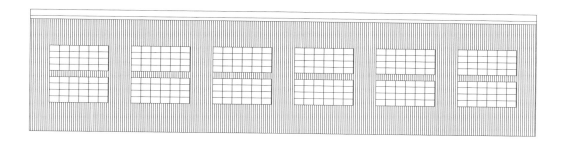

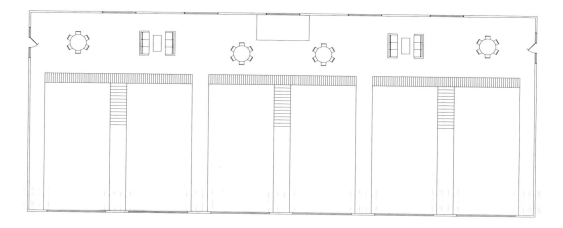

[(120) martha's vineyard house, 1990]

An antique barn and an industrial building
were advertised next to each other in the
local newspaper. Both were brought to the
site and erected.

[(130) tenement]

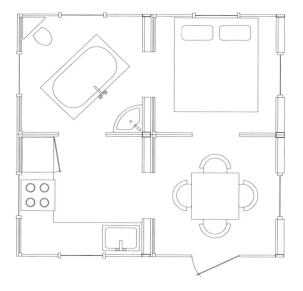

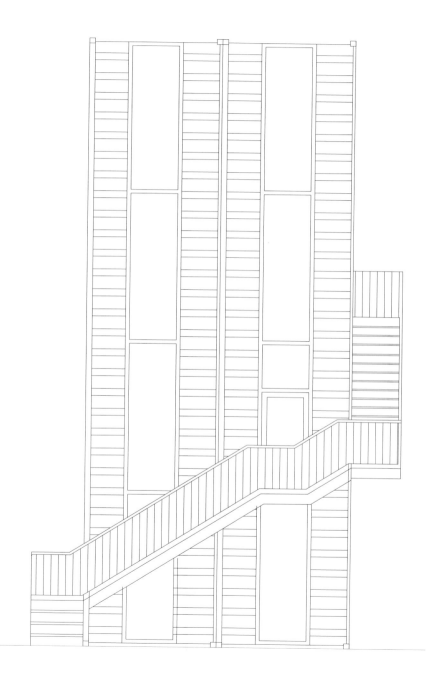

[(132) house for a monk]

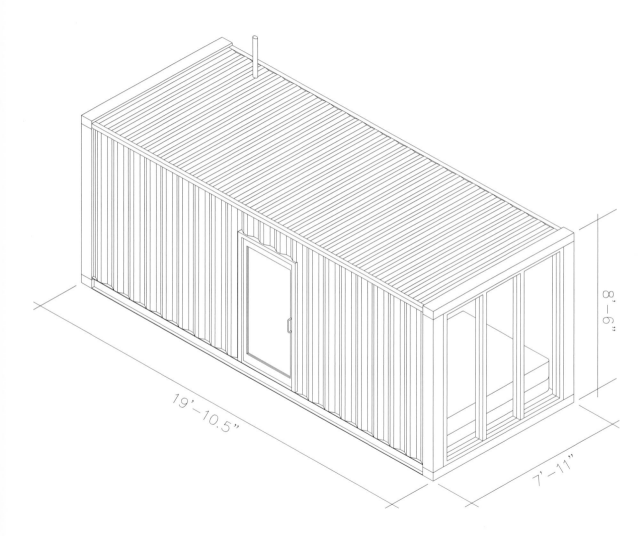

19'–10.5"

8'–6"

7'–11"

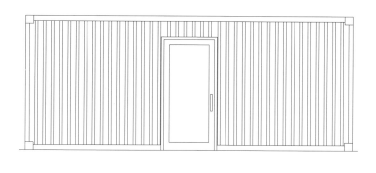

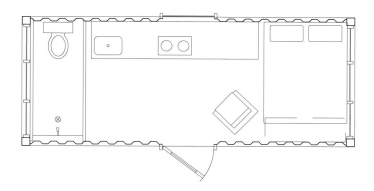

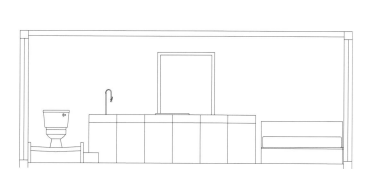

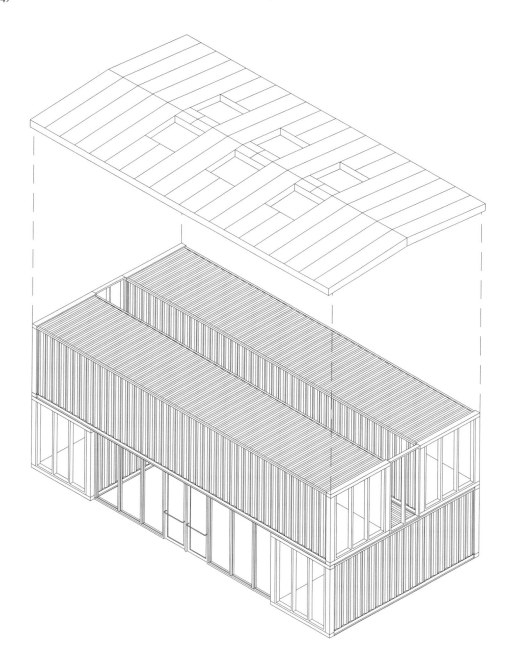

[(136)100 comments on architecture and hygiene]

1. Death is the punctus that consecrates all the arts and makes them work as a technology.
2. Architecture can be so many things; why is it so few things?
3. Why confine oneself to such a narrow aspect of the emotional spectrum?
4. I want to use the language of utility to create a kind of hyper-rationalized non-sense (see also: semantic incontinence).
5. Why does architecture dwell exclusively on the probable when it can dwell on the improbable?
6. What is risk in architecture?
7. Is architecture a useful tool for speculation? (How else can you build dreams exactly, point to them, weigh and measure them?) Architecture is the wordless exegesis of the dream.
8. Buildings are the result of a negotiated settlement: vulgarians on one side, hysterics on the other.
9. Someone said that by the time we are fifty, we have the face we deserve rather than the face we were born with.
10. I laughed in front of the judge.
11. Building is cogent violence, like surgery. Grass is the dermis.
12. The Interior is superior to the Exterior because it cannot be silhouetted and reduced to a visual field. What else swallows us whole? To be swallowed is the ideal sensual experience.
13. A coffin is a perfect house.
14. Cut the crusts off your bread!
15. Blues music is codified lamentation. Why is there not an architectural school of thought devoted to lamentation? Architecture is the perfect art to express suffering because it has consumed the most mortality in its making.
16. The 'I' is located in an interior space, inside the body. Is that the primordial architectural space?
17. Words are castrated Things.
18. Words beg for adjudication; buildings break the fall of a tree.
19. I prefer to think of architecture as the crust around a void.
20. Good architecture needs to overcome the gravity of our culture.
21. Robustness and morbidity: these are the polarities of architecture.
22. Lloyd Wright wanted to create an architecture based on landscape, but an architecture based on psychology is a far more intriguing proposition.
23. What happens to the architecture of the lecture hall when the speaker sits in the crowd?
24. Insects see opportunity in a fallen tree: true architects!

25. Some architects' discoveries amount to a new language, then there is hell to pay for the linguist.
26. If the architect is working properly, he doesn't know what he is doing.
27. How does the character of the idea (eidos) change as it suffers the indignities of worldly atmosphere?
28. Architecture should reflect the purple adjacencies in our lives.
29. How much anarchy is good for a building? A good architect courts anarchy.
30. In the U.S. postal system, each individual is associated with a place represented by an address. For 34 cents, the postman will draw a direct line between us. This is essentially an architectural idea.
31. What proportion of intelligence is vanity?
32. Imagine an entirely porcelain interior.
33. Without hygiene, architecture devolves to the jejune.
34. Polyphony? I consider it more a matter of smell.
35. The architect always tries to build his final building.
36. We are so sophisticated, we have no urgency.
37. Create problems if none exist.
38. Appliances are buildings.
39. Wittgenstein is an obsolete technology.
40. Politics is the perfect opposite of art.
41. The politics between individuals can be sublime, but the politics of groups is related to the technology of death.
42. What kind of advantage does the blind architect have over the sighted?
43. What does a key have to do with correctness?
44. Is figuration the quickest way to psychic frisson?
45. Foreign means unvisited.
46. Can there be a pathological architecture?
47. Most voices fall outside the frequency of architectural expression.
48. Architecture is a prodigious opportunity to sin.
49. What we say is confined by our embouchure.
50. Faith can only be arrived at through interpolation.
51. Speech is a social phenomenon; writing is an architectural one. Their histories, uses and physiognomies are unrelated.
52. The difference between language space and phenomenal space is only the density of the air.
53. Every building should have a pussy or other intra-oracular organ.
54. Unexplainably, Duchamp has made no impression on twentieth-century architecture.

55. Genius is a character flaw.
56. Try to be morally fastidious, but intellectually dishonest.
57. Architecture is a sub-set of sleep.
58. A policeman is a beautiful design.
59. In the city, the line between public and private becomes thin enough to vibrate with a poignant frequency (similar to the frequency of blue light in Chartres cathedral).
60. Every lie has had its own Darwinian struggle.
61. A newborn has the same fascinating ugliness as the city.
62. The architect always loses the battle of attrition with the human psyche which normalizes almost all experience.
63. Aging is characterized by increased schematization.
64. Misery is orthogonal.
65. Forgetting is the privilege of the individual; communities are perfect archives.
66. Vulgarity is a corollary of misery.
67. I am a male nurse.
68. What would music sound like if we could neither see, smell, touch nor taste?
69. Buildings can be infinitely long extrusions (i.e. pasta or string candy).
70. Genius is a form of hatred.
71. The half-life of an image is a peculiarity of its hygiene.
72. Architecture is under the tongue of language, sub-lingual, best expressed without the benefit of lips.
73. The witness is paid.
74. Moderation is part of the network of sensuality.
75. Contrary to intuition and practice, architecture should depart from a position of maximum risk. This is also the position of maximum hygiene.
76. Architecture is the circumscription of air.
77. Darwin had no sense of humor.
78. Ideas are formed by pressure; architecture is the redistribution of psychic pressure.
79. Who removed the clown from the mythology of architecture?
80. Utility is the servant of serendipity.
81. The threshold of the explicit is the altar of idolatry.
82. Jerry Lewis is an unsophisticated Kierkegaard.
83. Approach architecture as a 'What if...' proposition. Don't invest too heavily in its outcome.
84. It is difficult for me to distinguish between the art object and the fetish object. Perhaps the art object is becoming morally obsolete. It is a question of belief.
85. For me, buildings operate as surrogate bodies which I can contort, disguise, insult or embrace at will.

86. Glenn Gould has reinterpreted Bach so powerfully that he has achieved the status of co-author.
87. It is interesting that Gould could not really write any original music of his own. Interpretive intelligence is not necessarily impoverished creativity.
88. If you have no ideas, cut off a finger.
89. Creativity is not a desirable trait in a philosopher.
90. Does one consciously build a body of work or is it more a series of eructations?
91. Turn off your electricity for three days.
92. What is the semantic life-cycle of a building?
93. Photography thrillingly confuses truth and verisimilitude.
94. One does not need to understand biology in order to bear a child. In the same way, one need not understand phenomenology to produce a building.
95. The work is the search to reproduce and amplify a particular physical feeling in the artist.
96. Art is the provocation of memory.
97. Plans delineate political boundaries.
98. All authentic knowledge is sensual since it satisfies the desire to know.
99. Speech marks the cessation of thought.
100. Architecture engenders the threshold experience.

[(140) picture credits]

CAD images by Annan Mozeika and Chris Balasic
page 135 is based on a wallpaper design by Albert Hadley

Francois Dishinger: pages 8–11, 13–14, 17, 18, 22, 23
Durston Saylor: pages 12, 19, 34–36, 62, 63, 112, 118–126
Jaime Ardiles D'Arce/*Architectural Digest*: pages 38, 39
Peter Aaron/Esto: page 21
Peter Aaron/Esto/*Architectural Digest*: pages 74–81
Caelia Withers: pages 26, 30
Marjolein Boonstra: page 28
David Heald: pages 54, 55, 113
Ewald Timmermans: pages 92, 93
Tria Giovanni: page 111
Kalkin/Mik: pages 31, 50, 51
Kalkin/Mozeika: page 84
Kalkin/Balasic/Mozeika: pages 96, 97

Adam Kalkin's work is vertiginous in scope. It is driven by an inquisitive impulse coupled with an unencumbered sense of what is possible.

The houses that Adam builds embody the paradoxes, ambiguities, and ambivalences that are more often the domain of the art object than of the domestic environment. By appropriating the lexicon of the warehouse – Butler buildings, shipping containers, loading docks, industrial grating, concrete – he introduces an emotional ambiguity into an area of architecture that has long conformed to a limited set of effects. Neither conventional notions of comfort nor specific usage is encoded in the materials he uses or in the spaces he creates. His houses possess a layered interiority: found and reused structures create inner sanctums that recall childhood fortifications. The palatial volumes enclosed by his houses, together with the complexity of visual and visceral experiences they offer, make one feel that the spaces in which we live can themselves be transformative.

The work that Adam creates when not making buildings is equal parts performance, conceptual art, kinetic construction, and play. Dadaist in bloodline, his art is characterized by an inventive, low-tech, mechanized absurdity, informed by a handful of obsessions. At times there seems to be a spitting match going on between the outrageous and the sublime, but often they dance nicely together.

Adam Kalkin's art and architecture serve to dislodge any lingering tenets of either discipline that we may have inadvertently brought with us from the last century. Adam generates ideas that possess equal parts brilliance, innocence, and perversity, and he has achieved a high hit rate in realizing them.

Janie Cohen
January 2002

[(142) addiction]

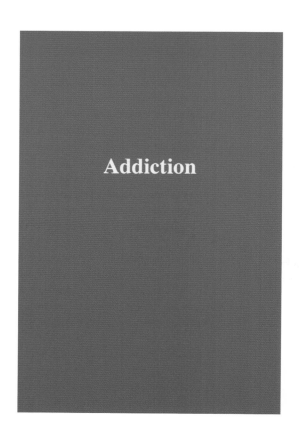

Addiction